JONAH
AND THE
BIG FISH

NINEVEH

Adapted by Tess Fries
Illustrated by Cheryl Mendenhall

Art Direction by
Shannon Osborne Thompson

All art and editorial material is owned by Dalmatian Press.
ISBN: 1-57759-522-X

11454a/Jonah and the Big Fish

01 02 03 LBM 10 9 8 7 6 5 4 3 2 1

Long ago there was a great city of Nineveh. The king and the people of Nineveh were very mean and did many things that made God unhappy. God decided to destroy the city. But He loved the people and wanted to give them a chance to change.

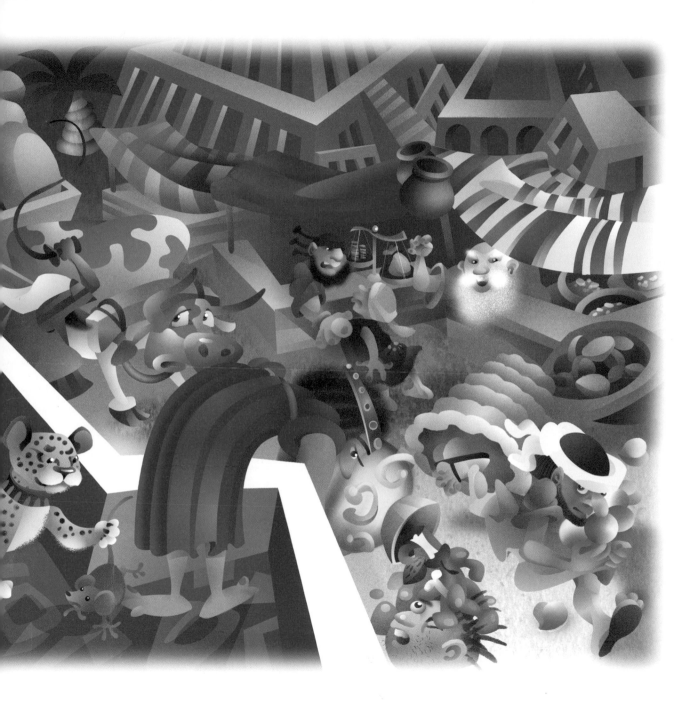

So God decided to send a man named Jonah to warn them that they must change. God told Jonah to go to Nineveh and tell all of the people of His plan.

But Jonah didn't obey. He ran to the sea and got on a ship that was sailing far away from Nineveh. He thought he could run away from God.

But God knew where Jonah was and He sent a fierce storm that caused the sea to be rough and rolling. The sailors were afraid. They called on their gods to quiet the storm but the winds blew harder and the waves grew higher.

They thought the boat would sink so they threw some of the ship's load overboard. But that didn't help.

All of this time Jonah had been sleeping in the bottom of the ship. The captain woke him up and said, "Get up and ask your God to save us—or we will drown!"

Jonah said to the terrified sailors, "Throw me overboard and the sea will become calm again. I know this storm has come because of me." The sailors didn't want to throw Jonah into the sea. They rowed and rowed, trying to get the ship safely to shore, but the storm only got worse.

Finally, the sailors knew they must do as Jonah requested. They picked Jonah up and threw him into the furious sea. Immediately, the wind stopped blowing, the sea became calm and the ship sailed away safely.

Jonah went deeper and deeper into the sea, but he didn't drown. God sent a huge fish to swallow Jonah whole. Jonah stayed in the belly of the fish for three days and nights.

Jonah was very frightened. He prayed to God from inside the fish. He was sorry he had disobeyed.

God listened to Jonah. He caused the fish to spit out Jonah onto the sandy beach. Then God told Jonah to go to the people of Nineveh and tell them what He had said.

The king of
Nineveh heard
Jonah's warnings
and was afraid. He
took off his royal
robes and put on
sackcloth and sat
in ashes. He told
his people to wear
sackcloth and to
tell God they were
sorry. The would
all start to do what
was right from
now on.

God did not punish the people of Nineveh because He loved them. He knew that they were truly sorry and wanted to do good from now on.

Everyday you choose between right and wrong. God wants you to make the right choice. Even when a choice seems too difficult, God will be there to help guide you.

*"But the LORD provided a great fish
to swallow Jonah, and Jonah was inside
the fish three days and three nights."
Jonah 1:17
(NIV)*